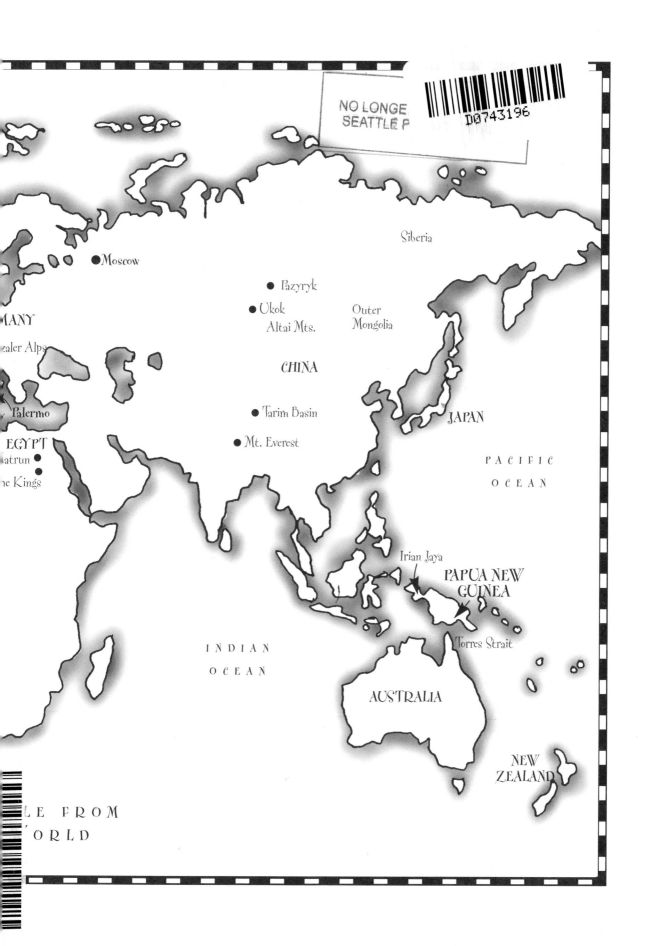

D0743196

Siberia

●Moscow

● Pazyryk

● Ukok
Altai Mts.

Outer
Mongolia

CHINA

●MANY

zaler Alps

● Palermo

EGYPT

atrun ●

he Kings ●

● Tarim Basin

● Mt. Everest

JAPAN

PACIFIC

OCEAN

Irian Jaya

PAPUA NEW
GUINEA

Torres Strait

INDIAN

OCEAN

AUSTRALIA

NEW
ZEALAND

LE FROM

ORLD

THE ENCYCLOPEDIA OF PRESERVED PEOPLE

Pickled, frozen, and mummified corpses from around the world

Natalie Jane Prior

Crown Publishers ♔ New York

Introduction

This is a book about people. It looks at men, women, and children from different times and many cultures whose bodies have been preserved until the present day. It is also about the archaeologists, historians, doctors, and other experts whose job it is to study the preserved bodies so we can understand how these people from the past lived and died.

Sometimes preserved bodies can tell us things a skeleton can't. Hairstyles and tattoos, like those found on the Greenland mummies and the Altai horse lords, give us an idea of what ancient people looked like. A full stomach, like Tollund Man's, can give information about what people ate. Autopsies and other tests can show what diseases people suffered from, what they died of, and even how they died.

Preserved people are fascinating because they allow us to look at the past face to face. When we can actually look at someone who was alive 100, 1,000, even 5,000 years ago, we realize that history is not about dull dates and facts but about people. People who laughed, cried, ate, worked, just like us. The study of preserved people helps point out the things that were different about their lives as well as the things that were the same.

How to use this book

This book has been written to be fun to dip into. However, some readers will also be looking for information about particular topics. The best way to find specific information quickly is to use the index at the back.

The Encyclopedia of Preserved People has two sections. The first one, "Preserved People Around the World," looks at individual bodies, types of bodies, and mummification methods from different continents, countries, and cultures. The second section, "Techniques, Tools, and Topics," has a series of short discussions of various subjects.

At the end of the book, a glossary explains unusual or difficult words. Words included in the glossary appear in **bold** type in the book.

Finally, if you would like to find out more about preserved people, there are many other excellent books about them. You can find information about some of these at the end of the book.

Preserved People Around the World

Preserved People of Africa

Some of the most famous preserved people in the world are the mummies of ancient Egypt. Egyptian mummies were among the first to be scientifically studied. Many of the techniques that are commonly used by researchers to study other preserved people, such as X rays, were first used on the mummies found in Egypt. Museums around the world often include Egyptian mummies in their collections.

amulets

An amulet is a piece of jewelry with a magical purpose, usually to protect the wearer. They were very popular in ancient Egypt. Living people wore amulets to protect them from danger in their daily lives, or if they were about to do something risky (such as go on a journey). When a person died, it was common for the embalmers to place amulets under the bandages as they wrapped the mummy.

Unfortunately, amulets did not always protect the mummy from attack. Because wealthy people often had amulets made out of gold and other precious materials, many mummies were broken up by greedy tomb robbers in search of treasure.

animal mummies

As well as human beings, the ancient Egyptians often mummified animals.

Most animals were mummified for religious reasons, because they were sacred to a particular god or goddess. For example, baboons and ibis were sacred to Thoth (the god of wisdom), crocodiles to

A mummified fish could be food in the afterlife.

A mummified donkey.

Sobek (the god of creation), and cats to Bastet (the goddess of the home). Priests at the god's shrine or temple would breed animals especially to be sacrificed by visitors. Sometimes this was done cruelly. While a cat might be lucky enough to be hit on the head, live birds were grabbed by the feet and plunged headfirst into vats of molten **resin**, where they boiled or burned to death.

In some cases, the spirit of the god was believed to live inside an animal with special markings, such as a bull. During its lifetime, the bull would be worshiped and cared for. Then on its death it would be mummified and buried in a special tomb.

Not all animals were mummified for religious reasons. Some were much-loved pets whose owners could not bear to leave them behind when they died. Mummified dogs, cats, monkeys, and gazelles have been found, wrapped in bandages and sleeping peacefully in the tombs of their owners. And archaeologists have also found mummified fish, ducks, and even joints of meat stowed in chop-shaped coffins—in case the human owner of the tomb woke up in the afterlife and fancied a snack.

bandages and bandaging

Most Egyptian mummies were wrapped in linen bandages. These strips of cloth were often recycled from old household linen, like sheets and tablecloths. Only very rich people could afford to use bandages that were especially woven.

Very early Egyptian mummies were not usually bandaged. But by the Archaic Period (3150–2686 B.C.), dead bodies were starting to be wrapped up in layers of cloth, probably because the embalmers thought the material would help preserve them. It didn't, but the embalmers soon

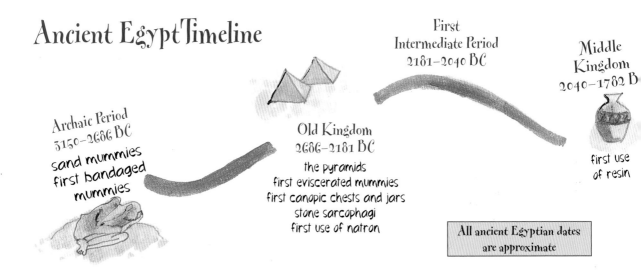

worked out techniques that did. They continued to use the bandages as they helped protect the dry, fragile mummy from damage and decay.

Bandaging was the last stage of the mummification process, and mummies were always wrapped with great ceremony and care. The bandaging began with the individual fingers and toes, followed by the limbs, the body, and finally the head. All the time, special prayers would be chanted and magic amulets would be slipped into the wrappings for protection. Sometimes hot resin would be used to seal the bandages around the body and keep the amulets in place.

Over the centuries, ways of wrapping mummies changed and became more elaborate. **Textile** experts can now tell where and when a mummy was made just by looking at the bandages. Some of the nicest bandaging was actually done after Egypt became part of the Roman Empire in 32 B.C. These Roman Period mummies have beautiful geometric patterns in the bandages. Unfortunately, by then many of the tricks used by earlier embalmers had been completely forgotten. Underneath the handsome wrappings, the Roman mummies are often badly preserved.

SEE ALSO: cerecloth (p. 54); unwrappings (p. 14)

Book of the Dead

The *Book of the Dead* is a collection of spells and prayers that was often written on a papyrus scroll and buried with dead Egyptians of the New Kingdom (1570–1070 B.C.). It was meant to be an instruction manual for the afterlife, explaining what the dead person should

Ancient Egypt Timeline

First
Intermediate Period
2181–2040 BC

Middle
Kingdom
2040–1782 B

Archaic Period
3150–2686 BC
sand mummies
first bandaged
mummies

Old Kingdom
2686–2181 BC
the pyramids
first eviscerated mummies
first canopic chests and jars
stone sarcophagi
first use of natron

first use
of resin

All ancient Egyptian dates
are approximate

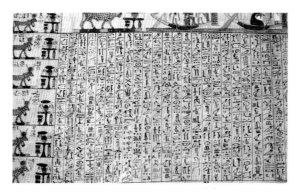

Hieroglyphic writing in a copy of the *Book of the Dead*.

The god Anubis judges a dead person by weighing his heart against a feather.

do and say when questioned by the gods about the life he or she had just left. If the instructions were followed and the right answers were given, the soul would reach eternal life.

Brier, Bob

Bob Brier is an American expert on mummies who has an unusual claim to fame. He is the first modern person to have embalmed a dead human body in the ancient Egyptian way. In 1994, after many years of research, he and a team of colleagues mummified the body of an elderly man at the University of Maryland. They used natron that was imported especially from Egypt, bronze embalming tools that were copies of tools found by archaeologists, and a stone knife to cut open the body.

Second Intermediate Period 1782–1570 BC

rule of Hyksos invaders

New Kingdom 1570–1070 BC

removal of brain through nose
The Book of the Dead
Valley of the Kings
reign of Tutankhamen (1334–1325 B.C.)

Third Intermediate Period 1069–525 BC

Late Period 525–352 BC

mummification goes into decline
Herodotus visits Egypt and writes about mummification

Graeco–Roman Period 352 BC–AD 641

reign of Alexander the Great (332–323 B.C.)
reign of Cleopatra, last queen of Egypt (51–30 B.C.)
wrappings become very elaborate
portrait masks become popular

The mummification was a success. When Bob Brier's team had finished with it, the dead body looked just like an ancient Egyptian mummy. It was placed in storage in a "tomb" at the medical school. Studies on the Maryland mummy are continuing, to see how it fares over time.

SEE ALSO: Egyptian mummies (p. 9)

canopic chests and jars

When an ancient Egyptian's dead body was embalmed, some of the **viscera** (internal organs) were removed as part of the process. These included the heart, liver, lungs, stomach, and intestines. The heart was usually preserved and replaced inside the body. The other organs were mummified separately.

This golden shrine protected the viscera of the pharaoh Tutankhamen.

At first, the mummified organs were placed in a special wooden chest, perhaps with four compartments inside for the individual packages. This chest (called a canopic chest) was normally placed at the foot of the **sarcophagus** when the body was buried. However, by the Middle Kingdom (2040–1782 B.C.), purpose-made jars, shaped a bit like thermos flasks, started becoming fashionable. The jars started off very plain, but later became quite fancy. Many jars had human or animal heads on the lids. The heads were those of the Four Sons of Horus, gods who were supposed to protect the jar's precious contents from damage or decay.

Sometimes canopic jars were placed for safekeeping inside a chest or box of their own. A pharaoh could have a whole shrine dedicated to protecting his viscera, like the one made of wood and gold that was found in Tutankhamen's tomb. All of this was expensive, however, and some people who wanted to save money simply had their mummified internal organs wrapped with bandages and left lying carefully at the foot of their coffin.

By the New Kingdom (1570–1070 B.C.), mummified organs were usually put back inside the body. However, the fashion for canopic jars did not die out, and many tombs have been found with empty jars in them.

Incidentally, if an ancient Egyptian time-traveled into the 21st century and were asked about his canopic jars, he wouldn't understand the question. The word "canopic" is originally Greek. It comes from the name Canopus, an ancient Greek god who was worshiped in the form of a jar.

Egyptian mummies

The ancient Egyptians first started preserving their dead about 5,000 years ago. They probably got the idea from the sand mummies that formed when bodies were buried in the desert on the west bank of the Nile. Early Egyptian mummies were just wrapped in bandages for protection, but the bodies rotted away under the bandages, and the embalmers soon realized that a more complicated method of preserving the body was needed.

Over the following centuries, the Egyptians worked out several methods of mummification for people with different budgets. The cheapest form was simply to cover the dead person with natron salt until the body had dried out. This is what happened to most Egyptians when they died. Others were injected with an **enema** of oil that dissolved the internal organs before drying out. Only very rich people could afford the best and most elaborate type of mummification, which took nearly three months to complete.

An Egyptian sand mummy, preserved in the hot sand without bandages.

Work began as soon as the corpse arrived at the embalmers' workshop. First, the body was washed and the internal organs removed. An implement like a crochet hook was poked up the nose to remove the brain (it was basically stirred to a mush and allowed to dribble out) while a specialist embalmer, called the "ripper up," carved a long slit in the side or groin and pulled out the intestines, liver, and other organs with his bare hand.

After the body cavity had been emptied, it was washed out and stuffed with straw, mud, rolls of material, or other packing. The face was painted with hot resin to protect it, and the body was covered with natron, a salt that naturally sucks moisture out of dead tissue. After about 40 days, when nothing was left of the body but a shriveled husk, it was taken out of the natron. It was then transferred to the *per nefer*, or "house of beauty," where the final preparations for burial took place.

The newly mummified body was not a pretty sight. It was dry, skinny, and bore hardly any resemblance to the living person it had once been. The last stages of mummification were aimed at improving the appearance of the body using sweet-smelling oils and makeup, and protecting it from damage with coatings of resin and bandages. Hot resin was painted over the body and magic amulets were placed on it for protection. The actual wrapping was done by special priests, who used strips of cloth supplied by the dead person's family. The wrapping could take more than two weeks and was accompanied by chants, prayers, and religious rituals.

SEE ALSO: amulets (p. 4); bandages and bandaging (p. 5); sand mummies (p. 61)

embalmers' caches

Ancient Egyptian embalmers had special tool kits that they used to prepare corpses for mummification. Because it was common for this equipment to be used only once, embalmers' tools were often

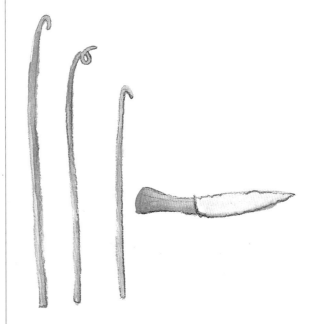

Hooks were used for removing the brain through the nose, and knives for making incisions.

buried with the mummy. Archaeologists call these tool kits embalmers' caches.

Equipment found in embalmers' caches includes bronze hooks (for removing brains), stone knives, bandages, and even the low-sloping table that the corpse lay on while the embalmers worked. This equipment has helped Egyptologists to understand exactly how mummification worked. The caches also include pots of natron, oil, and other ingredients used in the mummification process.

Guanche mummies

The Canaries are a group of islands in the Atlantic Ocean off the coast of northwestern Africa. For around 2,000 years, Tenerife, the largest island, was the home of the Guanche people. Important Guanches were mummified when they died and placed in dry burial caves.

Modern archaeologists think the Guanches used a mummification method similar to the ancient Egyptians'. They removed the internal organs from the body, stuffed it, and dried it. This was possibly done in the hot sun; however, it is difficult to know for sure. Mummification stopped when the Canary Islands became part of the Spanish Empire about 600 years ago. Within a short time, no one could remember how it was done, and since then most of the Guanche mummies have disappeared or been destroyed.

mumia

Mumia is an old Persian or Arabic word for bitumen, a black, sticky **tar** that

The Cambridge Guanche lived in the Canary Islands about 650 years ago. He was killed by a blow to the head with a heavy club.

looked a bit like the resin used by ancient Egyptian embalmers for coating mummies. Early travelers to Egypt thought that mummies were coated with bitumen, learned the word *mumia,* and started calling the embalmed bodies "mummies."

Because Middle Eastern doctors sometimes used *mumia* as a medicine, a rumor started that mummies—dead human bodies—were very good for sick people. Bodies that were thousands of years old started being taken back to Europe, where they were ground up and turned into medicine. "Mummy powder" for treating coughs and other illnesses could be found in European **apothecary** shops as late as the early 1800s.

natron

Natron is a salt that was used by the ancient Egyptians to dry out human bodies and turn them into mummies. It is mostly sodium bicarbonate (used by cooks to help cakes rise, and by people with indigestion to help bring up burps) and sodium chloride (the salt we put on our food). It was also used by the ancient Egyptians as a household cleaner, and in place of toothpaste.

The ancient Egyptians called natron *netjry,* which means "divine salt." Nobody knows for sure how they discovered that natron sucks moisture out of human tissues, but by the Old Kingdom (2686–2181 B.C.) embalmers were using

An artist's interpretation of an Egyptian wall painting, showing the dead body being covered in dry natron crystals.

it to prepare bodies for burial. The best and most expensive sort of mummification involved packing the body with natron, inside and out, for about 35–40 days. This was long enough for the body to dry out, without letting it fall to bits.

Ancient embalmers got most of their natron supplies from Wadi Natrun, a lake west of modern Cairo. Although dried natron can be found around the shores of the lake, early Egyptologists believed that natron was used in liquid form and that mummies were soaked in baths. In the 1930s, experiments with chickens proved that this idea was wrong. Only dry natron produced chicken mummies. Liquid natron made the flesh go sludgy and produced a decaying chicken soup.

SEE ALSO: Egyptian mummies (p. 9)

Tutankhamen

Tutankhamen's mummy is the most famous of all Egyptian mummies. However, it is not in very good condition. When it was finally unwrapped three years after the discovery of the pharaoh's marvelous intact tomb in 1922, it was something of a disappointment.

Tutankhamen died around 1325 B.C., when he was about 18 years old. (His skull is fractured, so he may have died in an accident, or even have been murdered.) Because he was so young and had not

Tutankhamen's mummy was enclosed in a sarcophagus and three mummiform coffins.

The entrance to Tutankhamen's tomb in the Valley of the Kings.

been expected to die for many years, his funeral had to be arranged in a hurry. A tomb was borrowed from someone else, and there was a rush to get all the **funerary equipment** organized. When the bandaged body was placed in the coffin, about 3 1/2 gallons of gooey, scented funeral oil was tipped over it. The oil soaked through the bandages, damaging the mummy's brittle flesh and turning it black. Then it set hard, gluing Tutankhamen into his coffin for the next 3,250 years.

This is the official story, put about at the time of the original unwrapping by the tomb's discoverer, Howard Carter. However, some experts now believe that the mummy was damaged even further by Carter himself. In order to de-glue Tutankhamen from his coffin, he left the mummy sitting in the Valley of the Kings for several hours so that the hot sun could soften the hardened oil. Unfortunately, he then wrenched it out of the coffin, breaking its arms, legs, feet, and head in the process.

SEE ALSO: Egyptian mummies (p. 9)

unwrappings

Egyptian mummies have been collected by museums and individual people for hundreds of years. Sometimes, however, the temptation to find out what is underneath the bandages is too much, and the mummies have been unwrapped.

In the 19th century, rich collectors would hold "unrollings" of mummies for their friends. Sometimes public mummy unwrappings were held, which people could pay to go and see. The unwrappings were done by people who claimed to be experts, but who did not know very much about what they were doing. Bandages were often taken off roughly, damaging or even destroying the mummy, and very little was learned in the process.

The first really scientific mummy unwrappings took place at the end of the 19th century. Experts unwrapping the bodies began to study them, trying to learn about how the mummy was made, what the dead person had been like, and what he or she died of. But because the bandages were stuck to the bodies, often with solidified resin, they were still badly damaged in the process, and many mummies were lost forever.

Today, mummies are hardly ever unwrapped. Modern medical techniques like X rays and CAT scans can tell researchers what is under the bandages without the need to remove them.

SEE ALSO: CAT scan (p. 53); X rays (p. 62)

Preserved People of
Australasia, Asia, and the Pacific

The very hot and often humid climates of many of the countries in Asia, Australasia, and the Pacific are not the best for preserving bodies indefinitely. In damp weather, bodies can rot or be attacked by fungus. Also, some cultures expect their mummies to last only a few years and use mummification techniques that don't last. Most of the best preserved and oldest corpses were actually preserved by accident.

Altai horse lords

More than 2,000 years ago, the Altai Mountains, on the border of Outer Mongolia and Siberia, were the home of tribes of horsemen. They roamed the grasslands with their herds, seeking out pastures and moving constantly from place to place.

The tribal rulers were wealthy people with many horses. When they died, they were buried in spectacular **barrows** called kurgans, which were covered with stones. Some of these tombs were excavated in the first half of the 20th century by a Russian archaeologist called Sergei Rudenko. He found the preserved bodies of several

This felt picture of a warrior on horseback was found on a wall hanging in a kurgan tomb.

tribal chiefs, who were covered with elaborate tattoos.

The people in the kurgan tombs had been mummified before they were buried. Their brains had been fished out through a hole cut in the back of their necks and their internal organs had been removed through a long slit in their sides. The bodies had then been stuffed with grass, embalmed with a mixture of spices, and buried under the mound at the bottom of a deep shaft. Moisture seeped into the tombs and froze solid, so that the bodies were preserved for about 2,400 years in blocks of ice.

Sadly, most of the kurgan burials had been attacked by tomb robbers. Treasure left in the graves had been stolen and the other contents damaged. But in the 1990s, another Russian archaeologist, Natalya Polosmak, found two unlooted tombs on the Ukok Plateau. One contained the tattooed mummy of a princess, buried in a coffin made out of a

log. The Ukok Princess, who was about 25 when she died, had been buried with expensive Chinese silk and wool clothes, a fancy wooden headdress, and other personal possessions. Around her grave were the skeletons of six horses, which had been killed and buried with her as a sign of her rank. The other tomb contained the mummy of a frozen warrior, with two long red plaits, high leather riding boots, a horse, and weapons. He had been killed in some sort of fight about 2,500 years before, when he was stabbed or gored in the stomach.

Australian Aboriginal mummies

A number of Australian Aboriginal peoples traditionally mummified their dead. This was done simply, by using the hot climate to naturally dry out the body. The dead person was tied in a sitting position and left out in the sun to dry. The body would then be placed in a tree or on a wooden platform. Sometimes, to speed up the process, a smoky fire was lit under the body while it lay on the platform.

Aboriginal peoples did not make a habit of preserving everyone who died. Mummification was usually reserved for a special person, like a leader or great warrior, or for people who died in special circumstances (for example, in a fight

against enemies). Unlike the Egyptians, Aboriginal people did not expect their mummies to last forever. After a while, when the grieving was over, mummified bodies were usually buried or otherwise disposed of.

Parts of Australia where dead Aboriginal people were sometimes mummified include the western Cape York Peninsula, Atherton Tablelands, and the Maranoa district in Queensland; Gippsland in Victoria; and the Adelaide

This 160-year-old picture shows dead Aboriginal warriors being smoke-dried on platforms.

Plains and Lower Murray River area in South Australia.

SEE ALSO: desiccation (p. 55); smoke-drying (p. 62)

Irian Jayan mummies

People from Irian Jaya (the western half of the island of New Guinea) mummified their dead until well into the 20th century. They did this by tying up dead bodies, propping them up in trees, and drying them with sunlight and sometimes smoke.

Irian Jayans kept mummies of dead relatives in their houses so they could remember them. For convenience, the mummies were usually dried in a crouched position, which meant they took up less space.

SEE ALSO: desiccation (p. 55); smoke-drying (p. 62)

Japanese monks

In Japan, Buddhist monks have been known to practice do-it-yourself mummification—starting the process while still alive!

The monks were members of a Buddhist sect that looked forward to the coming of a new Buddha, millions of years into the future. Because they wanted to help the Buddha when he came, they decided to remain on earth by preserving their bodies. Japanese experts who have

The candles around the Japanese monks drew moisture out of their dying bodies.

studied the monks' bodies are not completely sure how they went about doing this. However, it seems that the monks began their own mummification by gradually eating less and less. Their flesh slowly wasted away from their bones and they began to starve. Eventually, they stopped eating altogether and sat, surrounded by candles, until they died.

The candles were meant to draw moisture out of the monks' dying bodies. After death, the bodies were dried out further by the monks' companions and reverently stored in the local temple.

The process of turning oneself into a mummy was called *nyûjô*, which means "entering into Nirvana" (Nirvana is the

Buddhist equivalent of heaven). No one knows exactly how many monks became mummies, but it was probably quite a large number. *Nyûjô* was especially popular in the 11th and 12th centuries. However, because Japan's climate is a humid one, most of these very old bodies have fallen to pieces.

Today, the bodies of about 15 mummified monks survive in temples around Japan. The last monk to mummify himself, a man called Bukkai, died about 100 years ago, in 1903.

Lady Dai

In 1972, workmen building an underground military hospital at Mawangdui in Hunan, China, were startled to discover an ancient tomb that had been sealed for 2,100 years. Three graves at the foot of deep shafts contained the bodies of Chinese nobles, along with personal belongings and offerings of food. The best preserved of these is the famous Lady Ch'eng, wife of a Chinese nobleman, the Marquis of Dai.

Known today as "Lady Dai," the dead noblewoman had been wrapped in 20 layers of cloth, placed in a tightly fitting nest of six coffins, and buried in a wooden tomb at the bottom of a deep shaft. The elaborate burial shut out any **bacteria** that might have caused the body to decay. (It has also been suggested that Lady Dai was mummified in a bath of mercury salts.) Lady Dai's skin and hair were still intact, and her body was soft, like that of someone who had died only recently. In life, she had been a short, fat lady with bad lungs, gallstones, and a heart condition. In fact, she probably died of a heart attack after suffering from a bad case of indigestion. When doctors performed an autopsy, they found her intestines contained an incredible 138 melon seeds— the remains of Lady Dai's last pig-out.

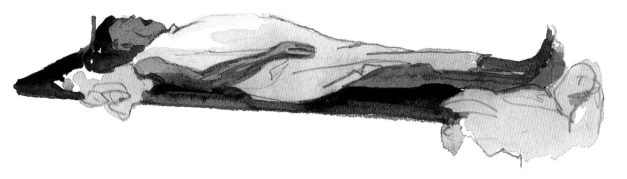

The body of "Lady Dai" was extremely well preserved, probably due to her elaborate burial.

Mallory, George

The first people to successfully climb Mount Everest—the world's tallest mountain—were Sir Edmund Hillary and Tenzing Norgay in 1953. However, they were not the first to make the attempt.

In May 1999, the frozen body of a famous English climber, George Mallory, was found on the North Face of Mount Everest. He and his companion, Andrew Irvine, had disappeared in 1924 while trying to reach the summit. Mallory's body was still dressed in the tweed climbing suit he had put on for the last time 75 years before, and his climbing rope was still tied around his waist. Name labels were sewn inside his clothes, and he had letters in his pocket from his family.

The mystery of Mallory's death was solved. He had fallen on the mountain, broken his leg, and injured his head. (The head injury was probably what killed him.) The historian of the expedition that discovered him believes he was on the way down when he died. But there is no way of telling how far up Mount Everest Mallory got before he fell. The mystery of who reached the summit of Everest first—Mallory and Irvine, or Hillary and Norgay—is still unsolved.

Torres Strait mummies

The people of the Torres Strait Islands, between Cape York in Queensland and Papua New Guinea, traditionally mummified corpses so they could keep dead relatives alongside the living. Like the ancient Egyptians, they fished out the brain, removed the internal organs from a slit in the side, and stuffed the body before drying it. The messy part of the mummification was usually done in a canoe, which was anchored off the shore of the island. Internal organs and any other waste were thrown overboard, and the body was tied to a wooden stretcher and hung up to dry for several months. The finished mummy would be decorated and kept by its relatives until eventually, after a number of years, it fell apart.

The best-known mummy of a Torres Strait Islander is the Macleay mummy. This mummy of a man had been shaved, dried, painted red, and given eyes made of

George Mallory's 1924 Everest expedition. Mallory is second from the left in the back row.

shells. It was collected off the coast of Papua New Guinea in 1875 and is now kept at the University of Sydney's Macleay Museum, though it is not on display.

SEE ALSO: desiccation (p. 55)

Xinjiang mummies

The mummies of the Tarim Basin in Xinjiang, China, are naturally preserved human bodies dating back as far as 6,000 years. The bodies were dried out when they were buried in hot, dry, sometimes salty soil. Over the years, several hundred mummies have been found, some of them looking much as they did when they were alive. However, it is not just their amazing state of preservation that makes these mummies interesting—it is what they can tell archaeologists about the way ancient peoples moved and settled along trade routes.

Although found in what is now China, many of the mummies are not Asian. They have Caucasian features with round eyes, pale skin, and light brown or fair hair. This means they may have originally come from somewhere in Europe. It seems possible that the people of the Tarim Basin first settled there when trade began between Europe and China along the famous trade route now known as the Silk Road. The age of the mummies also suggests that trade between Europe and

Mummy of a woman from the Tarim Basin.

Asia might have existed much earlier than historians realized. DNA tests are now being carried out on the mummies to try and work out exactly where they came from.

SEE ALSO: desiccation (p. 55); DNA testing (p. 56)

Preserved People of Europe

Many of the preserved people of Europe were preserved by accident. However, for centuries there was also a European tradition of embalming bodies, particularly those of kings, queens, and other important people.

Some European preserved people are still in remarkable condition after hundreds or even thousands of years. Quite a few, including the Ice Man and some of the famous bog bodies, can be seen today by the public in European museums.

Bentham, Jeremy

Jeremy Bentham (1748–1832) was a famous English philosopher. When he died, he left specific instructions about what was to happen to his body. Watched by his friends, it was to be dissected by doctors, then stuffed and put on display. Jeremy Bentham called this stuffed body his "auto-icon." He hoped that his example would set a trend, and that in future it would be commonplace for people to be turned into auto-icons when they died.

On his death, Jeremy Bentham's instructions were carefully carried out. His body was dissected by a surgeon, the skeleton reassembled, and the head embalmed. (Unfortunately, the finished head didn't look very attractive, so it was replaced by a wax one.) The auto-icon was then dressed in Jeremy Bentham's clothes and displayed at University College London. For many years afterward, it was taken out on special occasions so it could attend university meetings.

The auto-icon of Jeremy Bentham. His real head sits between his feet.

bog bodies

Bog bodies are preserved people found in northern European countries where peat bogs are common. Peat contains a substance called tannin, used in tanneries to make leather for shoes and other leather products. When a living or dead person falls or is pushed into a peat bog, the acid in the cold, peaty water kills the bacteria that would normally make a body rot away. Then the tannin in the peat acts on the skin and tissues, and effectively turns them into a "leather person."

A bog body has dark brown skin, clothes, and hair, the same color as the peat. Its face is not shriveled up like an Egyptian mummy's, but is often plump and lifelike. In many cases, the fingernails are still attached to the hands, and the fingerprints can still be seen on the fingertips. Sometimes the internal organs are still present, and archaeologists can tell what the person ate before they died. However, not all bog bodies are perfectly preserved. Some are crushed by the weight of the peat, and others are partially rotted away. Since very acid water makes bone slowly dissolve, other bog bodies are little more than a skin bag with no skeleton inside.

Some bog bodies were probably travelers who disappeared when they fell into bogs and drowned. But many Iron Age bodies, dating between 500 B.C. and A.D. 400, appear to have met more grisly ends. Bodies have been found stabbed, strangled, or with their throats cut. Then, after death, the executioner or murderer pushed the body into the bog and pinned it down with sticks or heavy stones.

Some of these people may have been murdered, or executed for crimes we can't know about. But some may have been human sacrifices, pushed into the bogs at the coldest, hungriest part of the year to please the mother goddess who made the

crops grow. Many bog bodies were young, attractive people (to give the goddess somebody old and sick would have been an insult). And most seem not to have struggled against their violent deaths. This may mean that they were drugged first—or it may mean they were volunteers who were happy to die.

Although bog bodies have been found in Europe for hundreds of years, it is only over the last 50 years or so that archaeologists have made a proper study of them. The following are some of the more famous ones:

Tollund Man

Tollund Man is the most famous bog body of all. His strangled body—naked, except for a little leather cap—was found in a Danish bog called Tollund Mose in 1950. Although parts of his body have decayed, Tollund Man's face looks almost as it had on the day of his death. Many people have commented on how peaceful he looks.

Tollund Man was the first bog body to be thoroughly studied by modern experts. His body was excavated and examined by the great Danish bog-body expert Peter Glob. But local people have never forgotten a sinister event that happened when the body was taken away for study. One of the men helping to recover the body collapsed and died of a heart attack. As Professor Glob later wrote, "The bog claimed a life for a life."

The most famous of all bog bodies, Tollund Man, with the rope that was used to strangle him.

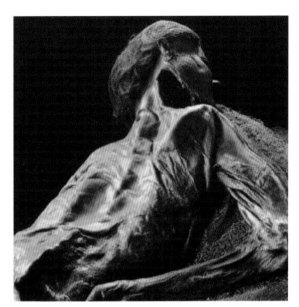

Grauballe Man was hit on the head and had his throat cut.

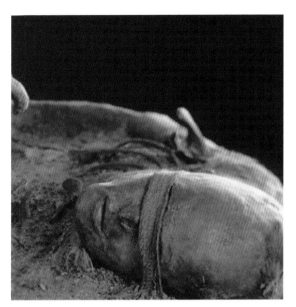

Windeby Girl was blindfolded and had her head shaved before she was killed.

Grauballe Man

Grauballe Man was found in 1952 in a bog called Nebelgård Fen, not far from Tollund Mose. Like Tollund Man, he died violently. Unlike Tollund Man, his body does not look peaceful. About 1,700 years ago, Grauballe Man was hit on the head and had his throat brutally slashed. The expression on his dead face is chilling.

Grauballe Man may have been a human sacrifice, though it is impossible to be sure. However, one of the oddest stories about his discovery relates to an old lady who lived locally. When the body was put on display, she caused a sensation by claiming his real name was Red Christian—and that she had played with him when she was a little girl!

Windeby Girl

Windeby Girl was very young when she died about 2,000 years ago—perhaps only 14 years old. Before she was pushed into the bog and drowned, her head was shaved and she was blindfolded with a red and yellow headband. The body was pinned down with a rock to stop it from floating back to the surface. Windeby Girl may have been executed as punishment for some crime she had committed, or she may have been a human sacrifice.

Lindow Woman

Lindow Woman is also known as Lindow I because she was the first bog body to be discovered in Lindow Moss, a peat bog in Cheshire, England. In fact, she is only a skull—but her discovery is famous because it helped solve a modern murder.

In 1960, a local woman called Malika Reyn-Bardt disappeared. Police were convinced her husband, Peter, had murdered her, but they had no body and no proof. Years later, when a skull turned up in Lindow Moss, they confronted Peter Reyn-Bardt. When he heard about the discovery, he confessed that he had killed Malika and buried her body in the Moss.

Needless to say, Lindow Woman was not Malika Reyn-Bardt. Archaeologists now think that the skull is around 1,740 years old—and that it is actually a man's! (It probably belongs to Lindow III, a mashed-up body found in 1987.) However, all this was too late for Peter Reyn-Bardt. Following his confession, he was convicted of his wife's murder and sentenced to life imprisonment.

SEE ALSO: Danish mound mummies (p. 28); Florida bog bodies (p. 39); peat and peat bogs (p. 61)

Lindow Man

In 1984, some English peat cutters working at Lindow Moss were startled to find a human foot caught in their machinery. They had discovered Lindow Man (also called Lindow II), the most famous of all English bog bodies.

Lindow Man probably died around

Lindow Man's body was so crushed it is hard to see his features.

2,000 years ago. Although he was badly crushed by the peat, and the bottom half of his body is mostly missing, archaeologists now know that he was a young, fit man with brown hair and a beard. Because he had smooth hands, he was probably an important person who did not have to work. He also died a particularly grisly death. Lindow Man was hit on the head, strangled, and had his throat cut before he was thrown into the bog—probably as a human sacrifice.

bog dogs

Preserved animals as well as people are sometimes found in European peat bogs. Bog dogs are especially common. Some are probably companion animals or working dogs who accidentally fell into

the bogs and were drowned. Others were killed and buried in the bogs for reasons we can't now be sure of.

Vets as well as archaeologists find bog dogs interesting, as they tell us about the sorts of dogs people bred and used in the past. One bog dog, found at Dreichsmoor in Germany, has short brown hair and was killed about 2,000 years ago. It looks rather like a dachshund—a breed of dog that has only been around for the last 100 years or so.

Bonaparte, Napoleon

Today, Napoleon Bonaparte is buried in Paris. But though tourists flock to see his elaborate tomb, it was not the first in

Napoleon Bonaparte as a young man.

which he was buried. When he died in 1821, the great general and emperor of the French was buried at St. Helena, a tiny island near the equator where he had been sent as an exile by his conquerors.

Nineteen years after his death, Napoleon's body was dug up so it could be taken back to France. St. Helena's hot climate should have caused Napoleon's body to decay quickly, so the men who exhumed him were expecting a skeleton. Instead, they were startled to discover that the emperor looked just as he had when he was buried.

Although he officially died of cancer, many people now believe Napoleon was murdered. On his death, his hair was shaved off and given away as keepsakes to friends and relations. Modern toxicologists (people who study poisons) have studied this hair and found it contains enormous quantities of arsenic, a deadly poison. It has been suggested that the arsenic was used to kill the emperor, and that it preserved his body from decay.

SEE ALSO: royal bodies (p. 35)

Catherine de Valois

Queen Catherine de Valois was a French princess, the wife of the English king Henry V. Although properly buried when she died in 1437, the queen's embalmed body was later dug up and left in an open

Samuel Pepys kissed the mouth of a queen who had been dead over 200 years.

coffin in Westminster Abbey, London, for more than 200 years. Sightseers gawked at her leathery skin and old-fashioned clothing, and one was even bolder. On a birthday outing in 1669, the diarist Samuel Pepys visited Queen Catherine and treated himself to a kiss!

SEE ALSO: royal bodies (p. 35)

Corder, William

The English murderer William Corder bashed and shot to death Maria Marten, his pregnant girlfriend, in 1828. He buried her body under the floor of a local barn, where it was found some months later by a gamekeeper.

The crime was so horrible that when the murderer was caught and hanged, people danced and cheered at his execution. But William Corder's punishment continued after his death. After his body was dissected by doctors, various bits of it were preserved. The local hospital got his skeleton, as well as his brain in a bottle, and a leather shop in London got his scalp and one of his ears. Finally, Corder's skin was tanned like cowhide and used to bind a book telling the story of his crime.

The Trial and Memoirs of William Corder, bound in the murderer's own skin, together with the scalp and ear, can still be seen in the Bury St. Edmund's Museum, England.

Danish mound mummies

Dead bodies can be buried in two ways: either by digging a hole in the ground and lowering the body or coffin into it or by heaping dirt or stones over the top of it in a mound. Several mound burials in Denmark have been found to contain preserved people. Over 3,000 years ago, the mound bodies had been placed in huge coffins made from hollowed-out oak trees. Sometimes, when water seeped into the oak coffins, it created a solution of tannic acid (similar to that used for tanning leather today). This turned the

A Danish mound mummy in its oaken coffin.

mound bodies into "leather people," a bit like the famous bog bodies found in the same area.

The most famous mound mummy was found at Egtved in central Denmark in 1921. It was a young woman with blond hair, dressed in a trendy string mini-skirt and woolen sweater. Unfortunately, her face had disappeared, but she must once have been wealthy and important. Not only were her hands smooth and well kept, she had taken her servant with her. The **cremated** remains of a young girl were found in the coffin with her—put to death so she could follow her mistress to the afterlife.

exploding kings and queens

Queen Elizabeth I was one of the most famous rulers England ever had, but her dead body caused an extremely embarrassing moment shortly before her funeral in 1603. One version of the story says that the queen insisted her body should not be embalmed; another version says that the queen was embalmed, but that the job was done badly. At any rate, the queen's two coffins—one wood, one lead—were left lying in state for more than a month after her death, with her body decaying inside. The buildup of gases inside her putrefying corpse eventually became so great that the body exploded and blew up both coffins!

Apparently, one of Queen Elizabeth's predecessors, William the Conqueror, nearly went the same way. At his funeral at Caen in France in 1087, the seal on the coffin gave way and "all the strength of the incense smoke could not prevent the congregation from hurrying out of the church, leaving the terror-stricken monks to finish the service as best they could." Much the same happened to another, much later, British ruler. When George IV died in 1830, his apothecary, John Nussey, was instructed to embalm the body. He wrote to his wife, Mary, that he did this "with his own hands," but since an apothecary was more a doctor than an

George IV was king of Great Britain from 1820 to 1830.

Royal apothecary John Nussey was the embalmer of King George IV of Great Britain.

undertaker, it seems he didn't do a very good job. While it was lying in state at Windsor Castle, the king's lead coffin was found to be so swollen and buckled from the putrefying gases inside that it had to be hastily punctured and resealed to stop it from bursting. An eyewitness remarked that it must have been a very unpleasant job.

The last story about an exploding royal concerns Mademoiselle de Montpensier, a cousin of France's most famous king, Louis XIV. After her death, her heart was taken out of her body for separate burial. It was placed in a small casket that obviously wasn't strong enough for the job. During the committal service at the church of St. Denis, the casket suddenly exploded with a loud bang. The smell was so awful all the mourners quickly ran away.

SEE ALSO: hearts (p. 59); royal bodies (p. 35)

Grottarossa mummy

The Grottarossa mummy is a very unusual preserved person from ancient Rome. It is the body of an eight-year-old girl that was embalmed by being coated in hot resin. The Grottarossa mummy is about 1,700 to 1,800 years old. The body, and the sarcophagus that contained it, were found by a garbage truck driver in a heap of fill being taken from a building site in

1964. The sarcophagus contained some of the girl's belongings, including jewelry and her favorite doll.

Ancient Romans did not usually preserve their dead. Although the dead little girl does not seem to have been an Egyptian herself, mummification by coating in resin was practiced in Egypt at this time. Archaeologists have suggested her family may once have lived in Egypt, or that they were followers of the ancient Egyptian religion.

The Ice Man (Ötzi)

The Ice Man is one of the most famous preserved people discovered in the 20th century. Found by hikers on the mountainous border of Austria and Italy, he froze to death around 5,000 years ago and fell into a hollow in the rock. His body was then dried out by the intense cold and remained buried in the ice of the Ötzaler Alps until September 1991. During the summer of that year, a cloud of dust blew across from the Sahara Desert and settled on the ice, causing it to melt and release the Ice Man from his frozen tomb.

Despite years of research, nobody really knows for sure who the Ice Man was or what he was doing in the Alps when he died. Various people have suggested he was a trader, a hunter, a shepherd taking

The Ice Man was found by hikers.

his flocks to winter pastures, or even a *shaman* (witch doctor). He was certainly well equipped for the journey, dressed in warm leather clothes, a grass cape, fur hat, and boots (stuffed with grass to help keep out the cold), and carrying food and weapons, including a bow and a beautiful copper ax. The copper ax was one of the most exciting finds, for it is the oldest ever found. It had been used by its owner to kill animals, including deer, not long before he died, which might explain what the Ice Man was doing.

At first, researchers thought Ötzi, as he was nicknamed, was about 25 years old, but it later turned out he was about 10 years older and in rather bad health. Stress marks on his fingernails prove he had been ill in the months before he died. He also suffered from arthritis and had tattoos on his back and behind his legs, which might have been spells to ward off pain.

In 1998, the Ice Man moved into his own museum in the Italian town of Bolzano, not far from where he was discovered. He is now on permanent display in a specially designed refrigerated room, which keeps him at a constant temperature of 43°F.

SEE ALSO: freeze-drying (p. 57)

Lenin, Vladimir Ilyich

Vladimir Ilyich Lenin (1870–1924) was one of the leaders of the Communist revolution that took over Russia in 1917. After his death in 1924, he was embalmed by some of Russia's top biochemists in a mixture of glycerine, potassium acetate, water, and quinine chloride. The result was so lifelike that his enemies claimed the body was only a wax dummy.

A glass coffin was built for Lenin's corpse and it was put on display in a special building in Moscow's Red Square. Loyal Communists would line up for hours to visit it. The body remained on show for many years, constantly

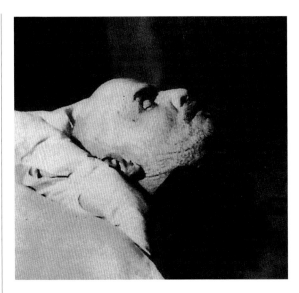

This photograph of Lenin was taken on his deathbed before he was embalmed.

monitored by the embalmers and occasionally being taken away for chemical treatments. After the collapse of Russian communism in 1989, it was taken off display.

Milton, John

John Milton was a famous English poet who lived from 1608 to 1674. In 1693, his grave in a local London churchyard was dug up and his well-preserved body was put on display by the church caretaker, a money-hungry lady called Elizabeth Grant.

Mrs. Grant charged visitors sixpence to see the dead poet. When the body started to rot and interest fell away, she reduced the admission charge to twopence.

John Milton's most famous poem was Paradise Lost.

After he died at the Battle of Trafalgar, Lord Nelson's pickled body was given a hero's funeral.

Nelson, Horatio

Horatio Nelson was a famous English admiral who led the British navy to victory in many battles. The greatest of these was the Battle of Trafalgar, fought against the French in 1805.

During the battle, Nelson was shot and carried belowdecks to die. Normally, he would have been buried at sea—sewn up in a canvas sheet with lead weights and dropped overboard. But because he was a great hero, it was decided his body had to go home. The only problem was getting it there. Trafalgar was off the coast of Spain, and the journey back to England would take a slow-sailing ship many weeks.

In the end, it was decided that the best thing to do with the admiral was to pickle him. After an autopsy, Nelson's hair was cut off and he was put into a wooden cask. The cask was then filled with brandy (some versions say rum), which stopped the body from rotting on the long journey home. Ever since, British sailors have called a drink of rum "tapping the admiral" or "Nelson's blood."

Palermo mummies

Some of the creepiest-looking mummies in existence can be seen at the monastery of the Capuchins at Palermo in Sicily. Here, over 8,000 mummies lie or stand upright in a series of underground catacombs. Many are monks, but most are ordinary people from the surrounding countryside, their shriveled heads and withered hands poking out of the Sunday-best clothes they were buried in.

Most of the Palermo mummies are natural ones. Sicily has a hot, dry climate, and new bodies were simply allowed to dry out, first in an underground room, then, after being washed in vinegar, in the sun. The oldest mummies in the collection are about 400 years old, but some are less than 100 years old. One tiny girl, who died in 1920 aged two years, is so lifelike she looks like she is sleeping. Unfortunately, no one today knows exactly why she is so well preserved—her father, the doctor who embalmed her, died soon after and took his secret with him.

SEE ALSO: desiccation (p. 55)

Henry VIII of England (above) had six wives. His last, Queen Katherine Parr, was buried upside down by drunken grave diggers.

Parr, Queen Katherine

Queen Katherine Parr was the sixth wife of King Henry VIII of England. In 1782, nearly 250 years after her death, the queen's body was accidentally dug up at Sudeley Castle in Gloucestershire. It had not decayed at all and became a local tourist attraction until it finally started to rot and smell.

Eventually, the queen's body deteriorated to the point where it had to be reburied. Unfortunately, the grave diggers were drunk and Queen Katherine was accidentally buried upside down.

SEE ALSO: royal bodies (p. 35)

Philip the Handsome

Philip the Handsome was a 16th-century ruler of a huge kingdom that took in parts of northern France, Belgium, and the Netherlands. His wife, Juana, was the queen of Castile (now in modern Spain). Queen Juana was wildly in love with her husband, who was famous for his striking good looks. Whenever he looked at other women, she became insanely jealous.

In 1506, Philip the Handsome died aged 28. Queen Juana went completely mad. She refused to allow her husband to be buried and kept his embalmed body in a coffin that she dragged around with her

wherever she went. People were horrified by the way she would take the body out of the coffin to cuddle and kiss it—especially as it eventually started to decay and fall apart.

Finally, the queen was persuaded to give her husband a proper burial. But although she lived for many years afterward, mad Queen Juana never recovered her wits and spent the rest of her life locked up in one of her palaces in Spain.

SEE ALSO: royal bodies (below)

royal bodies

Usually, the more famous and important you are, the more likely it is that your body will be embalmed. The bodies of kings, queens, princes, and princesses have always been preserved, often so that they could be taken long distances for burial. It was also important for the body of a reigning king or queen to be left out for a time, so that the monarch could be seen by many people to be truly dead. This stopped look-alikes from turning up and pretending to be the dead ruler and claiming the throne.

Many different methods of embalming have been used to preserve kings and queens. Most people know about the mummies of Egyptian pharaohs, but the Egyptians were not the only people to practice mummification. Alexander the Great, the famous ancient ruler, was preserved in honey when he died in Babylon (now in Iraq) nearly 2,400 years ago. He was taken to Egypt for burial, but unfortunately his tomb is now lost.

By the Middle Ages, the art of embalming kings and queens had become rather hit-or-miss. The job was normally done by the royal doctor, and some royals, such as the English kings Henry I and Henry V, were embalmed very sloppily

Henry V was sent back home to England for burial and was boiled down like soup!

indeed (Henry V was basically boiled into a soup; Henry I's doctor became so ill embalming the rotting corpse that he died himself). Other bodies, like those of the royal family of Naples in the 15th and 16th centuries, are still in excellent condition today. Their internal organs were removed and the flesh treated with resin to preserve it; the hot, dry climate of Naples also helped to dry out the royal corpses.

Kings and queens continued to be embalmed right up until the 20th century, though in Great Britain at least, the fashion finished with Queen Victoria. When she died in 1901, the queen left very definite instructions that her body was not to be embalmed (perhaps she'd heard what happened to her uncle, George IV; see "exploding kings and queens" on page 29). However, famous rulers such as Lenin in Russia, Chairman Mao in China, and Eva Peron in Argentina continued to be embalmed and placed on display right through the 20th century.

SEE ALSO: Bonaparte, Napoleon (p. 27); Catherine de Valois (p. 27); exploding kings and queens (p. 29); Lenin, Vladimir Ilyich (p. 32); Parr, Queen Katherine (p. 34); Peron, Eva (p. 50); Philip the Handsome (p. 34)

St. Bees Man

The body of St. Bees Man was found buried in a forgotten vault of a monastery church in northwestern England in 1981. He was about 40 years old when he died sometime after 1300. He had short brown hair, blue eyes, and a beard, all of which were remarkably well preserved.

St. Bees Man was a medieval knight, probably a **crusader** who had traveled to Israel to capture the holy city of Jerusalem for the Christians. His body was scarred from old fights, and he appeared to have died in battle. His jaw was freshly broken, and he had been speared or stabbed through the ribs. This second wound punctured his lung, which filled up with blood until he was unable to breathe, and he drowned in his own blood.

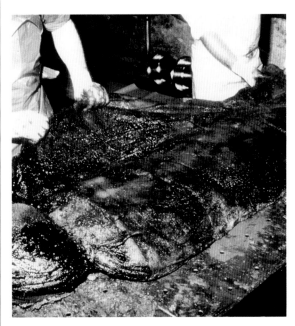

St. Bees Man in the process of being unwrapped.

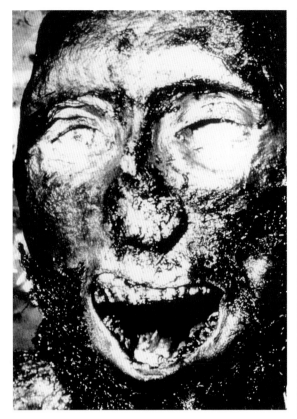

St. Bees Man's well-preserved face. His brown beard can easily be seen.

After his death, St. Bees Man was washed and wrapped tightly in two linen shrouds that were coated in resin. Then he was sealed in a body-shaped lead coffin. The sealed coffin and the tight wrappings around the body shut out all the bacteria that would normally cause the body to decay. St. Bees Man was so well preserved that when he was unwrapped, all his fingernails were still in place and his flesh was pink. When he was cut open during an autopsy, what appeared to be red blood flowed from the incision!

Botanists who studied the pollen grains found in St. Bees Man's coffin say they come from plants found only in Israel. This means St. Bees Man was brought all the way from Israel to England for burial, making him someone quite rich and important. While no one knows who he was for sure, he may have been the local landowner, Sir Anthony de Lucy of Cockermouth. St. Bees Man's body has now been respectfully returned to its original grave in the ruined church at St. Bees.

SEE ALSO: cerecloth (p. 54); shroud (p. 62)

Preserved People of
North America

North America is a large continent with a wide range of climates. Bog bodies, dried mummies, and frozen corpses have all been found there. There are also plenty of modern preserved people—some of whom have been preserved in unusual ways and for strange reasons!

Aleutian mummies

The Aleutian Islands are off the coast of Alaska in northwestern North America. About 500 to 600 years ago, the people who lived there started mummifying their dead. They did this by removing the internal organs and most of the body fat, stuffing the empty corpse with grass, and tying it in a bundle so it could be air-dried. To do this in the cold, damp Aleutian climate, the dead person's relatives needed to watch the body constantly and wipe away any signs of moisture while it desiccated. Sometimes heat from a fire was needed to help.

After the body was dried out, the dead person's relations would dress it and lay it to rest in a cave, warmed by a local volcano, where it would be safe in the warm, dry air. Mummification stopped in the 1700s when the Aleutian Islands became part of the Russian Empire.

SEE ALSO: desiccation (p. 55)

Einstein, Albert

The famous physicist Albert Einstein was born in Germany but lived in the United States for many years. When he died in 1955, his body was cremated after an autopsy. However, before this his brain

Albert Einstein's brain was eventually given back to his family after it had been pickled in a jar for many years.

was removed and kept (without his family's permission) by one of the doctors.

Einstein's brain was pickled in formaldehyde, supposedly so scientists could learn what made him so brilliant. Unfortunately, we still don't know—when the doctors examined it, Einstein's brain turned out to be just like anybody else's.

SEE ALSO: autopsy (p. 53); formaldehyde and formalin (p. 57); heads (p. 57)

embalming

Most modern Americans end up preserved whether they like it or not. This is because undertakers in the United States embalm practically everybody they prepare for burial.

While a few people have always wanted to be embalmed, the idea became popular in the United States after the Civil War, which was fought in the 1860s. Soldiers who were killed in battle were often embalmed so they could be safely shipped back home for burial. After the war was over, people got the idea that it would be healthier for living people if all corpses were embalmed. Today, most American dead bodies are embalmed, though it is not really necessary to do this.

Modern embalming is done with chemicals and is sometimes called arterial embalming. When a dead body arrives at the funeral parlor, the undertaker washes it with disinfectant and lays it on a special sloping table. An artery is opened and the blood and other body fluids are drained away. Then the blood is replaced with embalming fluid, which is a mixture of formaldehyde and wood alcohol.

Arterial embalming does not preserve a dead body forever. It simply slows down the process of decay so that the body will look nice before the funeral. This is helpful if relatives want to see the dead person before burial. However, it does not stop the body from eventually rotting away.

SEE ALSO: formaldehyde and formalin (p. 57)

Florida bog bodies

Although the most famous bog bodies come from countries like Denmark and

The body of a dead soldier being embalmed in a field hospital during the American Civil War.

Germany, Europe is not the only continent where bog people can be found.

The Florida bog bodies come from peat marshes in southeastern United States. The bodies—of prehistoric Indian people—are much older than the European bog bodies and, unlike them, are mostly of people who died natural deaths. Archaeologists believe they were buried in the marshes by their relatives. The bodies were carefully wrapped before burial and had been pinned down with stakes to stop them from floating to the surface. However, because they are so ancient—around 7,000 years old—they are not as well preserved as European bog bodies like Tollund Man or Windeby Girl.

Several "burial pools" have been found in the Florida **wetlands**, but only a few have been properly excavated by archaeologists. One pool, at Windover near Cape Canaveral, contained the bodies of over 160 people.

SEE ALSO: bog bodies (p. 23); peat and peat bogs (p. 61)

Franklin Expedition

In 1845, two ships, the *Erebus* and the *Terror,* set sail from England under the command of the famous Arctic explorer Sir John Franklin. They were headed on a voyage of exploration to find the Northwest Passage—a legendary route to the Pacific Ocean around the desolate icy coastline of northern Canada. At first, the two ships made good progress, but then they disappeared. Later, rescue missions discovered that the ships had been trapped in ice for 18 months. First the officers and then the crew had mysteriously started dying, until the last desperate sailors abandoned the ships and tried to walk to civilization. Many went crazy and some became so hungry they turned cannibal and ate their crewmates. All eventually perished—but no one knew exactly why.

In 1981, a Canadian **anthropologist** called Owen Beattie decided to investigate

Sir John Franklin headed up the 1845 expedition to the Northwest Passage.

the mystery of why the expedition had gone wrong. He went searching for bodies—not of the men who had starved in the ice, but of three sailors who had died very early in the expedition and who had been given a proper burial on Beechey Island in Lancaster Sound. Owen Beattie found the graves of William Braine, John Hartnell, and John Torrington and had the bodies dug up. Amazingly, after nearly 150 years the three men looked just as they had when they'd been buried. They had been frozen in the ice, about five feet below the ground, and every hair, fingernail, and eyelash was still in place.

All the sailors had died of natural causes, but their bodies were thin and weakened, which made Owen Beattie suspicious. Hair and tissue samples from out the best way of making the cans, and they were soldered shut with lead, which contaminated the food. On board ship, with no fresh meat or vegetables available, the sailors relied heavily on the deadly tins. Lead poisoning affects the brain as well as general health and can eventually kill. This was why some of the sailors had gone crazy, and why the officers, who ate more tinned meat, had died first. After 150 years, the mystery of the Franklin Expedition was solved.

Greenland mummies

In October 1972, two brothers called Hans and Jokum Grønvold found a couple of strange-looking rocks while out on a hunting expedition near Qilakitsoq (pronounced "krilakittork") on the icy western coast of Greenland. The brothers moved the stones and found two graves full of Inuit (Eskimo) mummies, freeze-dried by the cold, dry air for about 500 years.

The Grønvolds took photos and reported their find, but at first nobody was very interested in it. The mummies stayed where they were for five more years, until a new director, Jens Rosing, was appointed to the Greenland National Museum. One day, Jens Rosing was looking through a file when he happened to see the Grønvolds' photographs.

John Torrington, one of the sailors on the Franklin Expedition, was found in the Canadian Arctic almost 150 years after his death.

the bodies showed that all three men had suffered from lead poisoning, which they had contracted from eating tinned food.

In those days, tinned food was a very new idea. Factories had not yet worked

Amazed that such an important archaeological find had been ignored, he immediately sent a team of archaeologists to excavate the site. The eight mummies—six women, a small boy, and a baby—were carefully removed from their graves and flown to Copenhagen, in Denmark, for study.

This six-month-old Eskimo boy was found in Greenland in 1972. He died around 1475.

Because the bodies and their sealskin clothes were so beautifully preserved, it was decided that there should be no damaging autopsies. Despite this, the experts who studied the bodies in Copenhagen were able to learn a great deal from X rays and other non-invasive tests. For example, they found that one of the older women had cancer, which may have killed her. The small boy in the first grave probably suffered from **Down's syndrome** and may have been left out deliberately to die because he was crippled. (This seems cruel, but the Inuits' life was tough and they could not afford to support people who were unable to look after themselves.)

Another interesting experiment was performed by Niels Krømann, a Danish skin specialist. When he photographed the bodies with infrared film, he discovered that all the women except the youngest had elaborate tattoos on their faces. The tattoos, which probably meant that the women were married, were sewn into the skin with a bone needle dipped in soot. (This would have been excruciatingly painful.) Two women who had identical tattoos may have been sisters.

After the mummies had been thoroughly studied, the four best ones (including the baby) were treated with

gamma radiation to destroy any bacteria and fungus. Then they were sealed in airtight boxes and shipped back to Greenland for display in the National Museum.

SEE ALSO: freeze-drying (p. 57)

Little Al

Little Al is the mummified body of a small Woodland Indian boy who died about 200 years ago, aged around nine or 10. He was found in a cave in Kentucky in 1875, along with some moccasins, arrowheads, and other belongings. His discoverers thought he was a girl and called him Little Alice.

Little Alice became a sideshow attraction and was exhibited for many years in American fairgrounds as a child who had turned to stone. (In actual fact, the little boy's body had been dried out naturally in the cave.) Eventually, the mummy was retired from the fairground circuit and sent to the University of Kentucky for study.

This young woman lived on the west coast of Greenland about 500 years ago.

Preserved People of South America

South America is home to an amazing range of preserved people. For thousands of years, bodies were deliberately mummified by a number of South American cultures.

Some of the most interesting work currently being done on preserved people involves the remarkable "frozen children" discovered on high mountain peaks in the Andes mountain range.

Andean mummies

Some of the most exciting mummy finds from South America come from the Andes mountain range, which runs along the western side of the continent. The earliest discovery was made in 1954, when the frozen body of an eight-year-old "Inca prince" was found on a mountaintop near Santiago, in Chile. In the 1990s, a number of expeditions led by American archaeologist Johan Reinhard uncovered the preserved bodies of several children and teenagers, sacrificed to the gods around 500 years ago.

The frozen and freeze-dried bodies belonged to the Inca people, whose empire covered most of western South America in the 15th and 16th centuries. The most recent discoveries were made on several different mountain peaks in Peru and Argentina. Dressed in their finest clothes, the human sacrifices had been walked up the mountain to a sanctuary near the peak. Here, in a place that was sacred to the gods, they were drugged and then either hit over the head, strangled, or left to die of cold and exposure. A small girl and boy found by Johan Reinhard on a mountain called Nevado Ampato in 1995 were struck by lightning, while others were buried alive. All of them were young and healthy, and must have been children from well-off or even noble families.

Nobody knows why the young people were sacrificed. They may have been killed to stop eruptions of local volcanoes, or as part of a regular religious ritual. Offerings buried with the bodies include pottery, food, and small statues that were male or female depending on whether the sacrifice was a boy or a girl. Because some children have been found in boy-girl pairs, archaeologists have suggested that their deaths were supposed to represent the marriage of the god and goddess.

The Andean mummies are some of the best preserved ever found. Cloaks, sandals, and even spectacular feather headdresses have allowed experts to exactly reconstruct the way the Inca people wore their clothes. Because the bodies were frozen, not dried out, it should be possible to do DNA testing, which will help explain how the Inca are related to modern South American people. Also, stomach contents can tell us about diet, and medical tests give information about the general health of South American people 500 years ago.

SEE ALSO: DNA testing (p. 56); Inca mummies (p. 48); Juanita the Ice Lady (p. 48)

Chachapoya mummies

In 1996, some farmhands living in an isolated part of Peru noticed what seemed to be a small house in the forest above Laguna de los Cóndores (Condor Lake). After fighting their way through the forest, climbing rocks, and passing under waterfalls, they discovered an ancient Chachapoya burial village, lost in the misty Andes Mountains for 500 years.

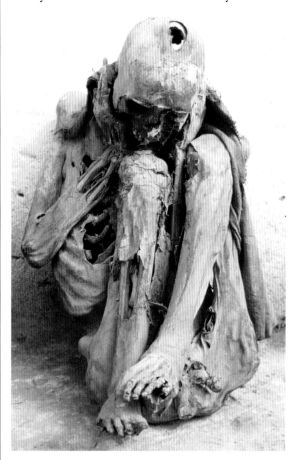

The hole in the skull of this Chachapoya mummy is due to an operation that the patient did not survive.

The Chachapoya people lived in northern Peru from about A.D. 800. They were tough and resourceful, but this was not enough to save them from their enemies, the neighboring Incas, who conquered them around 1470. The burial village above Condor Lake probably dates from shortly after this time.

Like the ancient Egyptians, the Chachapoyas tried to preserve their dead by mummifying them. All the bodies in the burial village were embalmed (probably by smoking them) with their knees and arms tied tightly under their chins. Cloth was wrapped and sewn around them until they looked like mailbags. Finally, the people who had prepared them for burial had embroidered smiling faces on the front of the mummies and placed them in special stone burial houses, or *chullpas*.

A whole village of *chullpas,* decorated red and yellow, had been built on a ledge of rock high above Condor Lake. The air here was cold and dry—a perfect environment for keeping mummies well preserved. Inside each *chullpa,* families of mummies rested comfortably on wooden platforms about five feet above the floor. Food and belongings were placed in the houses with them, and living relatives would visit them from time to time to make offerings and pay their respects.

Chachapoya mummies were wrapped in cloth bundles with embroidered faces.

Unfortunately, the Chachapoyas' 20th-century descendants were not so respectful. The men who discovered the mummies above the lake unwrapped the bodies, vandalized the *chullpas,* and stole the ancient belongings inside them. By the time they were caught and punished, hardly anything was left as they had found it. Archaeologists are still trying to piece the site and the mummies back together so they can study them.

SEE ALSO: Inca mummies (p. 48); Peruvian mummies (p. 51); smoke-drying (p. 62)

Chinchorro mummies

Ancient South Americans may even have been the first people to have deliberately mummified their dead. Mummies found at Chinchorro, in northern Chile, date back 7,000 years—at least 2,000 years before the first ancient Egyptian mummies.

The Chinchorro people removed the internal organs and stuffed the bodies. They took off the arms and legs, then re-attached them and coated the bodies with clay.

This Chinchorro mummy's face is coated with clay.

Copper mummy

Found in Chile in 1899, the Copper Mummy is a most unusual preserved person. The body of a copper miner who died in a mine collapse about 1,200 years ago, he was preserved by a combination of dry air and the copper salts in the earth that surrounded him. His dried-out, green body can be seen in New York, in the American Museum of Natural History.

Inca mummies

Between 1438 and 1572, the Inca Empire covered most of western South America. Its rulers were called, simply, the Inca. On their death, Inca rulers were mummified, wrapped in expensive shrouds, and then treated with as much respect as when they were alive. They were given living servants to look after them, feed them, and even bathe them! On special occasions, such as religious festivals, the royal mummies were brought out and paraded before their subjects before being returned to their tombs.

SEE ALSO: Andean mummies (p. 45); Juanita the Ice Lady (below); shroud (p. 62)

Juanita the Ice Lady

The most famous of the Andean ice mummies is a 14-year-old girl known as Juanita. She was found by accident on a mountain in Peru called Nevado Ampato

The Copper Mummy was the victim of a copper mine collapse around A.D. 1800.

Juanita the Ice Lady was really only a teenager when she died.

in 1995, after her tomb had broken and slid down the slope in a landslide. Because of the danger of losing the body altogether, archaeologists Johan Reinhard and Miguel Zárate had to carry it down the mountain on their backs and rush it 100 miles by public transport to the nearest freezer.

Juanita had been killed by a savage blow to the right side of her head. Her face had been dried out by the sun and wind, but her body was frozen solid. When found, one hand was still clutching the edge of her cloak in a death grip that had lasted 500 years.

SEE ALSO: Andean mummies (p. 45); Inca mummies (p. 48)

Mexican mummies

Parts of Mexico have a very hot, dry climate, which causes bodies to mummify naturally when they are left in the open air. In Guanajuato, north of Mexico City, mummies of local people are left buried in the town cemetery as long as the family members are prepared to pay a burial fee. When the fee stops being paid, they are dug up and put on display in an underground crypt. The Guanajuato Museum, featuring the mummified bodies of hundreds of men, women, children, and even babies, has become a famous local tourist attraction.

Another "Mexican" preserved person is Emperor Maximilian I. Maximilian was an Austrian archduke who was foisted as a ruler on the Mexicans by Emperor Napoleon III of France. He was shot by a firing squad in 1867 and stuffed by local **taxidermists**.

SEE ALSO: desiccation (p. 55)

Eva Peron as a young woman. After her death in 1952, her embalmed body was displayed to the public.

Peron, Eva

Eva Peron was the wife of Argentinian dictator Juan Peron. Today, she is best known outside her homeland as the subject of the famous musical *Evita* by Andrew Lloyd Webber and Tim Rice, but in her lifetime the poor people of Argentina regarded her almost as a saint. The story of what happened to Evita's body after her death is just as incredible as her life.

Evita died in 1952 of cancer, aged 33. Her heartbroken widower soon arranged

for a Spanish **pathologist**, Dr. Pedro Ara, to embalm her body. First, Dr. Ara stabilized Evita's corpse so it could lie in state. Millions of Argentinians came to see her in Buenos Aires, lying like Snow White in a glass-topped coffin. Then the body was taken away, soaked in chemical baths, and injected with paraffin. The bill for the embalming grew and grew, eventually reaching millions of dollars in today's money. Meanwhile, work started on a huge tomb where Evita's glamorous corpse could be put on permanent display.

After a year's work, the embalming was complete. The result was incredible: Evita looked just as she had when she was alive. But before she could be laid in her tomb, disaster struck. Juan Peron was overthrown, and he was eventually forced to leave Argentina.

To the new government, Evita's embalmed body was an embarrassment. They smuggled it out of the country and, after many adventures, it was eventually buried in Europe under a false name. Here it stayed until 1971, when supporters of the Perons kidnapped and killed Juan Peron's replacement, the former Argentinian president Pedro Eugenio Aramburu.

The kidnappers held Aramburu's body for ransom. The price for its return, they said, was Evita's. By then, hardly anyone knew where she was, but eventually her preserved corpse was tracked down to Milan, in Italy. Evita was dug up and returned to her husband, who kept her on display in his dining room for the next two years. Eventually, after Juan Peron died in 1974, Evita was flown back to Argentina and put back on public display for the last time, 22 years after her death. She now lies in a cemetery in Buenos Aires—in what is hopefully a burglar-proof vault.

Peruvian mummies

While Peru is famous for mummies like Juanita the Ice Lady, which were accidentally preserved, ancient Peruvian peoples sometimes mummified their dead deliberately. Depending on where or when they were made, the mummies were preserved by being dried out or smoked, or by using methods that are not really understood by modern archaeologists. Many Peruvian mummies were placed in a crouching position and tied up in a cloth bundle for protection—much as the ancient Egyptians wrapped their mummies in bandages. In most ancient Peruvian cultures, being mummified was a mark of respect.

SEE ALSO: Andean mummies (p. 45); Chachapoya mummies (p. 46); Inca mummies (p. 48)

Techniques, Tools, and Topics

autopsy

An autopsy (or postmortem) is a medical examination of a dead body, usually held to discover what the person died of, and sometimes to identify who he or she was. It is performed by a specialist doctor called a forensic pathologist. When the corpse is a preserved person from the past, it is performed by a **paleopathologist**, who has experience with ancient corpses, skeletons, and mummies.

In a typical autopsy, the pathologist will carefully examine the outside of the body, photograph it, measure it, weigh it, and X-ray it. Then he or she will cut the corpse open to examine the internal organs. Sometimes samples such as blood, tissue, and stomach contents will be taken away for further investigation. Afterward, the body is sewn up and given back to the family for burial or cremation.

In the case of a mummy or other preserved person, a full autopsy like this is often difficult to perform. The body is likely to be fragile and would be damaged or destroyed by cutting it open. In this case, the pathologists have to decide whether or not an autopsy would be worth it. Often they decide against it and use X rays, endoscopies, and other tests that will not cause any damage.

SEE ALSO: CAT scan (p. 53); endoscope (p. 56); X rays (p. 62)

cabinets of curiosities

Cabinets of curiosities were collections of strange and unusual objects made by rich Europeans in the 18th century. The collections were usually kept in large and elaborate cabinets or small rooms (also called cabinets) so they could be shown to guests or other interested collectors.

Depending on what the collector was interested in, a cabinet of curiosities could contain fossils, mineral samples, historical curios, and freaks from the animal and vegetable kingdoms. Some collectors with a ghoulish turn of mind would collect bits of bodies—including human and animal mummies and mummy parts, boxes of human teeth, and even deformed dead babies in bottles.

CAT scan

A CAT scan is a modern medical procedure that allows doctors to see inside a living or dead body. (CAT stands for computerized axial tomography.) A special machine takes a series of X rays of the part of the body being studied. These are then reassembled by a computer to give a three-dimensional picture.

CAT scans are very useful for studying preserved people because they mean fragile, irreplaceable bodies no longer have to be cut up.

SEE ALSO: X rays (p. 62)

cerecloth

A cerecloth was a special cloth used for wrapping dead bodies. Cerecloths were made of linen treated with wax (*cera* is the Latin word for wax). Because they were expensive, they were only used by rich people. The richer the person, the bigger the cloth: some wealthy medieval people had cerecloths that were wrapped around their bodies up to 12 times! The head and foot ends of the cloth were tied off, making the dead person look a bit like a piece of wrapped candy.

Because the wax helped keep out the damp and the cerecloth often filled the air spaces in a coffin, cerecloths sometimes helped preserve dead bodies by shutting out the bacteria that cause decay.

SEE ALSO: bandages and bandaging (p. 5); shroud (p. 62); St. Bees Man (p. 36)

coffins, caskets, and sarcophagi

The container a body is stored or buried in sometimes helps preserve it from decay by shutting out air and, with it, the bacteria that cause decay.

Body containers are usually made out of wood, stone, types of cardboard, or metal (particularly lead, which is soft, easy to work, and doesn't rust). They have changed a lot over the years, from simple coffins made out of hollow logs to elaborate sarcophagi used by Egyptian pharaohs to the plain varnished caskets and coffins of the present day. Nowadays, the word "coffin" usually refers to a trapezoid-shaped box that bulges out at the dead person's shoulders, while "casket" refers to a rectangular one. A sarcophagus (the plural is sarcophagi) is made out of stone, and may have one or more coffins nested inside it.

Despite what many people think, fancy, expensive, or even multiple coffins are no guarantee that the body inside will not decay. If a body survives inside a well-sealed, tight-fitting coffin, it is usually by a lucky accident.

cryonics

Cryonics is the practice of freezing dead bodies, in the hope that one day someone will be able to bring them back to life. The idea is an American one and dates back to the 1960s. For a fee, people can pay a cryonics company to collect their body as soon as they die and have it frozen in liquid **nitrogen**. (It is important to freeze the body as quickly as possible so that it does not start to deteriorate.)

Because this process is quite expensive, some customers freeze just their head. These people hope that some future doctor will be able to attach their head to another body, or grow them a new one to order.

decay

As soon as a person dies, the body immediately starts to change. The blood drains away to the lowest part of the corpse, causing blotches on the skin, while the rest of the body turns pale and goes stiff and cold. The first insects quickly arrive to lay their eggs, which will hatch into hungry maggots that consume the flesh. Bacteria get to work inside the body, starting the process of putrefaction, or decay.

After a day or so, depending on the temperature and where it is, the decaying corpse starts to turn a greenish color. It smells unpleasant and gas starts to form inside, making it swell up. After a few weeks, the skin splits and the internal organs dissolve. Eventually, all the flesh disappears and nothing is left but a skeleton.

Because decomposing bodies look and smell so awful, human beings tend to think of decay as being rather nasty. Over thousands of years, this has led to many people and cultures trying to find ways of preserving their dead for a short time, or even for eternity. While some of these methods have worked better than others, decay is actually a normal and necessary part of living. It is nature's way of cleaning up, making room, and providing food for living creatures.

desiccation

Desiccation means to dry thoroughly or suck moisture out. Human bodies are largely made up of moisture, and when this is removed, the tissue is preserved—much as plums are preserved by turning them into prunes, or apricots into dried fruit.

Human bodies are desiccated in several different ways. Sometimes, if the climate is hot and dry for long enough, it just happens naturally. Bodies can be desiccated in hot sunshine, in warm, dry caves, or when they are buried in hot, dry sand or earth. Sometimes bodies are artificially desiccated. Egyptian mummies were dried out using natron, a salt that sucks water out of human flesh.

SEE ALSO: Egyptian mummies (p. 9); sand mummies (p. 61)

disease

One of the most important things researchers study when they examine a preserved body from the past is the state of the dead person's health.

The study of ancient diseases is called paleopathology. A paleopathologist usually has medical, biological, or other scientific training and will work with archaeologists to study skeletons and bodies, perform autopsies, and conduct other medical tests, such as X rays, blood

tests, and endoscopies. They are not just curious to know what the preserved person died of. Studying ancient bodies helps historians and archaeologists learn a great deal about the way people lived in the past. Wear on teeth, for example, shows what people ate and whether their diets were good or bad. Injuries on battlefield victims tell us what weapons were used in wars. Studies of cemeteries give us an idea of how long ancient people might generally have expected to live.

Ancient corpses also help doctors and other medical researchers study the history of medicine. They can learn about how ancient people performed operations, set bones, and treated diseases that have affected human beings up to the present day. They can also better understand the way diseases change as they are passed from one person to another over centuries or thousands of years.

SEE ALSO: autopsy (p. 53); CAT scan (p. 53); endoscope (p. 56); X rays (p. 62)

DNA testing

All living creatures, including humans, have a unique code. This code is called DNA (short for deoxyribonucleic acid). DNA is found in the genes that exist in the nucleus, or heart, of every cell in our bodies. Every person's DNA is different, but because we inherit characteristics from our parents, we share some of our DNA with other members of our families.

The study of human DNA is useful for many things, including the study of preserved people. Geneticists (people who study genes) are now able to extract DNA from the cells of human beings who lived thousands of years ago. Very old DNA is called ancient DNA or aDNA for short. Studying it can show how a preserved person like the Ice Man, found on the border of Austria and Italy, is related to modern people from those countries. It can also prove whether a group of mummies (like the royal mummies of Egypt) are related to one another.

endoscope

An endoscope is a tiny camera on the end of a slender tube. Doctors use them to see inside the bodies of living humans—for example, to check whether somebody has a stomach ulcer or cancer.

Endoscopes are often used in the study of preserved people because they allow one to see inside a body without cutting it open. An endoscope can see inside the empty skull of an Egyptian pharaoh, or into the stomach of a bog person.

Some endoscopes are even able to take biopsies—tiny tissue samples from within the body, which can be used later for separate study.

Modern endoscopes are portable and can be taken to archaeological digs so that bodies can be examined where they are found. They are also used to see into coffins or tombs, giving archaeologists a sneak preview of their discoveries.

formaldehyde and formalin

Formaldehyde and formalin are chemicals sometimes used for preserving bodies, body parts, and scientific specimens. Formaldehyde was discovered in Germany about 140 years ago and began to be used as an embalming fluid in the early 20th century. Because it is a gas at room temperature, it is usually used dissolved in water. Formalin is a mixture of water, formaldehyde, and methyl alcohol.

SEE ALSO: Einstein, Albert (p. 38)

freeze-drying

Sometimes in very dry, cold conditions, mummies are preserved by freeze-drying. When this happens, the cold prevents the body from rotting while the moisture is slowly sucked from the tissues. (To get a good idea of how this works, look at a piece of meat that has been left for a while uncovered in the freezer.) Examples of freeze-dried mummies include the Ice Man and the Greenland mummies.

SEE ALSO: Greenland mummies (p. 42); Ice Man (p. 31)

gibbet

A gibbet is a cage shaped like a human body and hung from a scaffold. In some European countries, gibbets were placed beside busy roads and used to display the bodies of hanged criminals.

The dead body was coated with tar to slow down decay and hold it together, then placed inside the gibbet. Not surprisingly, it looked (and smelled) ghastly. Denying the dead criminal a proper burial was a way of continuing the punishment after death. And the sight of the horrid thing dangling by the roadside was supposed to frighten other criminals into behaving.

When the last two bodies were gibbeted in England in 1832, the event was seen by over 20,000 people. These spectators were simply ghouls who were certainly not learning a lesson from what they saw. Soon after this, the British government abolished gibbets for good.

heads

There are many examples of severed heads being preserved without the rest of the body. Often when a traitor or criminal was executed, his or her head would be preserved (sometimes by coating it in tar; sometimes by boiling it with salt and cumin, a herb that tastes bad to birds) and placed in a prominent spot, such as on a

bridge or castle battlement. One famous person this happened to was Sir (also Saint) Thomas More, the chancellor of King Henry VIII of England. More had his head chopped off for disagreeing with the king. It was speared on a pole and placed on London Bridge, until his daughter Margaret rowed down the river in the dead of night and rescued it.

Sometimes heads were preserved for other reasons. After the famous Austrian composer Joseph Haydn died in 1809, his body was dug up and his head cut off by a group of phrenologists. Phrenology was the 19th-century craze in which "experts" claimed to be able to predict a person's personality and intelligence by feeling the bumps on their skulls. The Austrian phrenologists who dug up Haydn were sure that the bumps on the head of a musical genius would be particularly interesting. They weren't, and it was over 150 years before the composer's head and body were reunited.

SEE ALSO: cryonics (p. 54); Einstein, Albert (p. 38)

head-hunting

Head-hunting is the practice of collecting the head of a dead enemy and keeping it as a trophy or relic. Many cultures have practiced head-hunting, including the ancient Celts in Europe, some South Pacific island cultures, and a number of Indian tribes in South and Central America. (Some North American Indian peoples collected and preserved the scalps of their dead enemies, rather than the whole head.)

Some headhunters, like those in the South Pacific, were happy to let heads decay until they were left with a grisly collection of skulls. Others went to great pains to preserve the heads, so they looked the same as they had in life. The reasons for wanting the heads varied, but usually a collection of heads gave the owner great prestige, and sometimes power over the dead enemy's spirit.

The ancient Celts would cut off the heads of their enemies in battle, then take them home and preserve them in cedar oil. Enemies' heads were also set into the gateposts of Celtic forts. Another people who traditionally collected the heads of enemies to gloat over after a battle were the New Zealand Maori. They called these preserved heads *mokomokai*. However, the Maoris also kept the heads of family members and friends for a different reason—as a sad way of remembering a lost loved one. Sometimes Maori warriors returned home with the heads of their own fallen relations, because this way they could stop them from falling into the hands of enemies.

head-shrinking

The most complicated method of preserving a severed head was to shrink it. The following method was used by warriors of the Jivaro tribe of Ecuador until the 1960s. They believed that it imprisoned the soul of the dead enemy inside the head, so it would not be able to come after the person who had killed it.

First, a slit was made in the back of the head. The scalp and face were carefully peeled away from the skull and jawbone and tanned in hot water for about two hours. When the tanning was finished, the eyes, the mouth, and the slit at the back of the head were sewn up, and the empty head was filled with heated stones.

The heat from the stones slowly drew the moisture out of the tissues, and the head began to shrink. As the stones cooled, they were replaced with a series of smaller ones until the head was hardly bigger than the headshrinker's fist.

The last step was to cure the head by smoking it. The head was filled with sand and hung over a slow fire. The finished head—called a *tsantsa*—could then be oiled, painted, and added to the head-hunter's collection.

hearts

Sometimes, when it is not practical to preserve a whole body, the heart is taken out and preserved separately. Because a heart is small, it can be easily sent home for burial if a person dies away from home. It can be buried separately if the person wanted to be interred in two different places, or it can even be kept as a gruesome souvenir if the dead person's relatives feel like it.

One person who asked for his heart to be preserved was King Robert the Bruce of Scotland. When he died in 1329, he asked that his heart be buried in far-off Jerusalem—a place he had always hoped to visit. (Unfortunately, the heart only got as far as Spain.) And the writer Mary Shelley (best known for her horror novel *Frankenstein*) kept her dead husband's heart as a memento, wrapped up in a piece of silk. (The heart was actually snatched out of the fire by a friend while the body was being cremated!) Her son later inherited it and would sometimes show it to friends as a special treat. (One ungrateful relation complained that it looked like a bit of old boot leather.)

The worst story about a preserved heart concerns King Louis XIV of France, who died in 1715. Eighty years later, during the French Revolution, his grave was robbed and the heart sold to an Englishman. It ended up in the possession of a very strange man called Francis Buckland, who was famous for eating

anything and everything—including Louis XIV's heart.

SEE ALSO: exploding kings and queens (p. 29)

jade

Jade is a beautiful gemstone that comes in many colors, but that is most frequently green or greenish blue. It is regarded as magical or powerful by many peoples from around the world, including the Maori people of New Zealand and the Chinese, who have used it for amulets and talismans for thousands of years.

Ancient Chinese rulers were sometimes buried entirely encased in jade. One such king was Liu Sheng, who ruled south of modern Beijing about 1,900 years ago. The graves of Liu Sheng and his wife, Dou Wan, were found by archaeologists in 1968. They had both been buried in jade suits of armor, made of 2,500 tiny jade pieces and wired together with pure gold. The jade's magical properties were supposed to preserve Liu Sheng and Dou Wan's bodies forever, but by the time their graves were discovered, both had completely rotted away.

The Maya people of Central America also believed jade had magical properties. They sometimes buried their rulers with jade face masks to ensure they lived forever.

SEE ALSO: amulets (p. 4)

mammoths

Mammoths were huge, woolly elephant-like animals that became extinct at the end of the ice ages 10,000 years ago. From time to time, frozen mammoths, which are tens of thousands of years old, have been discovered in the icy wastes of Siberia. (Most recently, two mammoths were found in 1978.) One mammoth, found in 1900, was in such good condition that the local people cut it up and fed it to their dogs! Its stuffed skin is now on display in St. Petersburg, Russia.

movies and books

Everybody loves a mummy, so it's hardly surprising that mummies (usually Egyptian ones) are favorite characters in movies and books. Sometimes the mummy comes to life; sometimes it's just there to add color and interest to the setting. One thing's for sure: no book or film set in ancient Egypt would be complete without one!

The most popular mummy movie ever made was an early horror film called *The Mummy*. It was made by Universal Pictures in 1932 and starred the actor Boris Karloff, who was famous for playing creepy roles. (He also played Frankenstein's monster in *Frankenstein*.) Imitations and remakes of it have appeared ever since (most recently in 1999 and 2001).

Living people falling in love with mummies and dead mummies magically coming back to life are the two most common themes in mummy books and movies. A number of famous novels have also been written about mummies. Probably the best known are *The Romance of a Mummy* by French writer Théophile Gautier (1857), which is about a young Frenchman falling in love with a mummy, and *The Jewel of Seven Stars* by Irish writer Bram Stoker (1903), about an ancient Egyptian queen returning to life. (Bram Stoker is more famous for having written *Dracula*.) The most popular late-20th-century mummy novel, *The Mummy, or Ramses the Damned* (1989), by American horror novelist Anne Rice, tells the story of a long-dead Egyptian pharaoh falling in love with a 20th-century woman.

peat and peat bogs

Peat is ancient, decayed plant matter that packs down over centuries and looks like very dark brown, sticky soil. It is often found in the potting mixes used by modern gardeners. Peat also burns easily, making a slow, rather smelly fire. In places like Ireland, where peat is cheaply dug up, it is used as fuel for cooking and heating.

In some parts of the world, especially in cold northern European countries like Denmark, Ireland, England, Germany, and the Netherlands, peat bogs are common. Peat bogs are marshes that contain lots of peat, and they can be spooky, dangerous places. Because the peat holds so much water, the ground underfoot can be sticky and treacherous. What looks like solid ground is often just a tuft of grass floating on a sea of muddy sludge. Unwary travelers can lose their footing and disappear forever, sucked under by the bog and drowned.

sand mummies

Sand mummies are natural mummies formed when a human body is buried in hot sand. Dry heat from the sand draws the moisture out of the body's tissues and it becomes desiccated and wrinkled, like a piece of dried fruit. Many sand mummies have formed accidentally, but some have resulted when a corpse is deliberately buried in hot sand.

Sand mummies have been found in many hot, dry countries, including Mexico, Australia, and Egypt. Ancient Egyptians buried their dead in the desert, on the west bank of the Nile, so they could save the precious green strip along the Nile River for crops and living people. The earliest Egyptian mummies are sand mummies that were probably preserved by accident over 5,000 years ago.

The most famous Egyptian sand mummy is a 5,100-year-old man now nicknamed Ginger because of his reddish hair. He can be seen in the British Museum in London.

SEE ALSO: desiccation (p. 55); Egyptian mummies (p. 9)

shroud

A shroud is a piece of cloth used to wrap up a dead body. Long shrouds are sometimes called winding sheets because they are wound around the body.

In the past, shrouds were often made of linen or other plain, tough fabrics, though poor people might have used an old sheet or other piece of material. Often the corpse was not placed in a coffin, and since the shroud was the only covering, the body would be sewn into it.

In medieval England, a law said that everyone had to be buried in a woolen shroud. This was not because woolen shrouds were better—it was to help the local wool industry!

SEE ALSO: bandages and bandaging (p. 5); cerecloth (p. 54)

smoke-drying

Dead bodies can be preserved by smoke-drying them—just like the smoked fish or chicken sold in delicatessens. The body or body part is positioned above a slow, smoky fire and turned occasionally over several days. (Sometimes the internal organs, which decay more rapidly, are removed first.) The heat draws out the moisture and the smoke cures the flesh.

Smoke-drying has been used by people in Peru, northern Australia, and the Torres Strait, and by headhunters in Ecuador.

SEE ALSO: Australian Aboriginal mummies (p. 17); head-hunting (p. 58); Torres Strait mummies (p. 20)

X rays

X rays are often used in the study of mummies, bog men, and other preserved people. X rays can show **tumors**, broken bones, or old injuries, just as in a living person. They can help prove how old a person was at the time of death. X rays are particularly useful because a body can be studied without unwrapping it or damaging it through an autopsy. Archaeologists have even used X rays to discover jewelry and amulets hidden in a mummy's wrappings.

The first person to use X rays on mummies was the famous English archaeologist Sir Flinders Petrie, in 1898.

SEE ALSO: CAT scan (p. 53); endoscope (p. 56)

Glossary

anthropologist
A person who studies human cultures and civilizations.

apothecary
An early medical attendant, somewhere between a modern doctor and pharmacist. Apothecaries treated patients as doctors would, but often had shops that sold drugs as well.

bacteria
Invisible organisms with only one cell. They can cause diseases, as well as make things decay.

barrow
A tomb where the earth is heaped up in a mound over the dead person's body.

cremation
Disposing of a body by burning it.

crusader
Someone who fought in the Crusades, a series of wars that were held in the Middle Ages in what is now Israel. Christian people from Western Europe tried to capture Jerusalem because it was a holy city associated with Jesus.

Down's syndrome
People with Down's syndrome are born with 47 chromosomes in every cell, instead of the usual 46 (chromosomes carry the genes that we inherit from our parents, the "blueprints" that make us who we are). People with Down's syndrome can be mentally retarded and suffer physical disabilities.

enema
An injection of liquid into the anus. Enemas are often given to people with bad constipation.

funerary equipment
Belongings and equipment buried with a dead person.

nitrogen
A gas that makes up most of Earth's atmosphere. When it becomes very cold, it becomes liquid and can be used to freeze things.

paleopathologist
Someone who studies ancient diseases.

pathologist
Someone who studies diseases.

resin
A sticky liquid that comes from trees, including cedars, firs, and pines. It was used by the ancient Egyptians for coating mummies.

sarcophagus (sarcophagi)
A stone container for holding a body and sometimes a coffin as well.

tar
A thick, black, sticky liquid that comes from treating coal.

taxidermist
A person who stuffs the bodies of dead animals so they can be put on display.

textile
Woven material or cloth.

tumor
A growth or lump. Sometimes, but not always, a cancer.

viscera
The organs (for example, heart, liver, kidney) inside a person's body.

wetlands
Swamps and boggy areas.

For more information

There are many excellent books about preserved people, some of which you are sure to find in your local library or bookshop. Here are a few titles you might find especially interesting. Books written for adults (but that will still be interesting for kids) are marked with an asterisk (*).

Beattie, Owen, and John Geiger. *Buried in the Ice: The Mystery of a Lost Arctic Expedition.* Toronto: Ashton Scholastic, 1992.

* Brier, Bob. *Encyclopedia of Mummies.* New York: Facts on File, 1998.

* Brothwell, Don. *The Bog Man and the Archaeology of People.* Boston: Harvard University Press, 1987.

Colman, Penny. *Corpses, Coffins, and Crypts: A History of Burial.* New York: Henry Holt & Company, 1997.

* Dunand, Françoise, and Roger Lichtenberg. *Mummies: A Voyage Through Eternity.* New York: Harry N. Abrams, 1994.

* Glob, P. V. *The Bog People: Iron-Age Man Preserved.* London: Faber, 1969.

* Partridge, Robert B. *Faces of Pharaohs: Royal Mummies and Coffins from Ancient Thebes.* London: BCA, 1994.

Perl, Lila. *Mummies, Tombs, and Treasure: Secrets of Ancient Egypt.* Boston: Clarion Books, 1987.

Prior, Natalie Jane. *Bog Bodies, Mummies and Curious Corpses.* Sydney: Allen and Unwin, 1994.

Putnam, James. *Eyewitness: Mummy.* Sydney: OK Publishing, 2000.

Index

A

Aleutian mummies 38
Alexander the Great 35
Altai horse lords 15–17
amulets 4, 6, 10, 62
Andean mummies 45–46
  Juanita the Ice Lady
    48–50
  see also Inca mummies
animal mummies
  bog dogs 26–27
  Egyptian 4–5
Australian Aboriginal
  mummies 17–18
autopsy 38–39, 43, 53,
  55, 62

B

bandaging 5–6
  cerecloth 54
  shroud 62
Beattie, Owen 41–42
Bentham, Jeremy 22
bog bodies
  European 23–26
  Florida 39–41
Bonaparte, Napoleon 27
Book of the Dead 6–7
Brier, Bob 7–8

C

cabinets of curiosities 53
canopic chests and jars
  8–9
Carter, Howard 14
CAT scans 14, 53
Chachapoya mummies
  46–47
Chinchorro mummies 48

coffins 54
Copper mummy 48, 49
Corder, William 28
cryonics 54

D

Danish mound mummies
  28–29
decay 55
desiccation 17, 18, 20,
  21, 34, 38, 50, 55,
  61–62
disease 55–56
DNA testing 21, 46, 56

E

Einstein, Albert 38–39
embalmers' caches 10–11
embalming 39
endoscope (or endoscopies)
  53, 56–57

F

formaldehyde and
  formalin 39, 57
Franklin Expedition
  41–42
freeze-drying 31–32,
  42–43, 45, 54, 57

G

gibbet 57
Glob, Peter 24
gods, ancient 4–5, 8–9,
  23, 45–46
Grauballe Man 25
Greenland mummies
  42–44
Grottarossa mummy
  30–31
Guanajuato Museum 50
Guanche mummies 11

H

Haydn, Joseph 58
head-hunting 58, 59
head-shrinking 59

I

Ice Man 31–32
Inca mummies 48–50
  see also Andean
    mummies
Inuit mummies 42–44
Irian Jayan mummies 18

J

jade 60
Japanese monks 18–19
Juanita the Ice Lady *see*
  Andean mummies

K

kings and queens
  Catherine de Valois,
    Queen of England
    27–28
  Elizabeth I, Queen of
    England 29
  George IV, King of
    Great Britain 29–30
  Henry I, King of
    England 35–36
  Henry V, King of
    England 35–36
  Juana, Queen of Castile
    34–35
  Katherine Parr, Queen
    of England 34
  Louis XIV, King of
    France 59–60
  Maximilian I, Emperor
    of Mexico 50

  Philip the Handsome,
    King of Castile and
    Archduke of Austria
    34–35
  Robert the Bruce, King
    of Scotland 59
  Victoria, Queen of
    Great Britain 36
  William the
    Conqueror, King of
    England 29
kurgan tombs 15–17

L

Lady Dai (Lady Ch'eng)
  19
Lenin, Vladimir Ilyich 32
Lindow Man 26
Lindow Woman 25–26
Little Al 44

M

Macleay mummy 20–21
Mallory, George 20
mammoths 60
Maori people 58, 60
Maryland mummy 8
Maya people 60
Mexican mummies 50
Milton, John 32
Montpensier,
  Mademoiselle de 30
More, Sir Thomas 58
Mount Everest 20
movies and books 60–61

N

natron 12–13
Nelson, Horatio 33

O

Ötzi *see* Ice Man

P

Palermo mummies 33–34
peat and peat bogs
  23–26, 40–41, 61
Pepys, Samuel 28
Peron, Eva 50–51
Peruvian mummies 51
  see also Chachapoya
    mummies; Juanita
    the Ice Lady
Petrie, Sir Flinders 62

R

Reinhard, Johan 45, 49

S

sand mummies 9, 61–62
smoke-drying 17, 18, 47,
  59, 62
St. Bees Man 36–37

T

Tarim Basin mummies 21
Tollund Man 24
Torres Strait mummies
  20–21
Tutankhamen 7, 13–14

U

Ukok Princess 17
unwrappings 14

W

Windeby Girl 25

X

Xinjiang mummies 21
X rays 14, 43, 53, 55, 62

Photo credits

The author and publisher would like to thank the following sources for assistance with respect to copyrighted material. Every effort has been made to trace and acknowledge copyright. The publishers apologize for any accidental infringement and welcome information that would rectify any error or omission in subsequent editions.

American Museum of Natural History, New York (49, top); Archäologisches Landesmuseum, Schleswig, Germany (25, right); Beacon Heritage Attraction, Whitehaven, England (36, 37); Bonniers/Moesgaard Museum, Denmark (25, left); British Museum, London, England (26); David Coltheart (5, 7, 8, 9, 13); Enrico Ferorelli (48); Greenland National Museum and Archives (43, 44); Keith Muscutt (46); *National Geographic* magazine (49, bottom); National Museum of Denmark (29); Novosti Photo Library (16); Silkeborg Museum, Denmark (24); South Australian Museum (17); Paul Stokes (11); University College London (23).

Cover image: *National Geographic* magazine

The St. Bees Man's shroud can be seen at the Priory Church, St. Bees, Cumbria, England. You can find out more on www.copelandbc.gov.uk.

Library of Congress Cataloging-in-Publication Data
Prior, Natalie Jane, 1963–
    The encyclopedia of preserved people : pickled, frozen, and mummified corpses from around
the world / Natalie Jane Prior.
        p. cm.
    SUMMARY: An encyclopedia of facts about preserved people from around the world, including
Egyptian mummies, bog bodies, Einstein's brain, and the Ice Man.
    Includes bibliographical references and index.
    ISBN 0-375-82287-9 (trade) — ISBN 0-375-92287-3 (lib. bdg.)
    1. Human remains (Archaeology)—Encyclopedias, Juvenile. 2. Mummies—Encyclopedias,
Juvenile. 3. Dead—Encyclopedias, Juvenile. [1. Human remains (Archaeology)—Encyclopedias.
2. Mummies—Encyclopedias. 3. Dead—Encyclopedias.] I. Title.

CC79.5.H85 P75 2003
393.3'03—dc21
                                                                                    2002019308

Printed in China
First Crown edition: March 2003
10 9 8 7 6 5 4 3 2 1

Picture credits appear on page 64.

Beechy Island

GREENLAND

Qilakitsoq

Alaska

CANADA

UNITED STATES OF
AMERICA

Kentucky

MEXICO

Windover

Florida

Guanajuato

ATLANTIC

OCEAN

UNITED   St. Bees
KINGDOM

London
FRANCE

SPAIN

Canary Islands

PACIFIC

OCEAN

Condor Lake

PERU

Mt. Ampato

Chinchorro

CHILE

Andes Mts.

ARGENTINA

Santiago

Buenos Aires

St. He

PRESERVE

AROUND